Reflections Of A Small Town Santa:

A *True* Story About Santa Claus

by Bob Litak

BLUE SKY MARKETING INC.
PO Box 21583-S, St. Paul, MN 55121 USA

Reflections Of A Small Town Santa:
A True Story About Santa Claus

Copyright © 1997 by Robert E. Litak
Just B. Claus Productions
PO Box 902, Cedarburg, WI 53012
Fax (414) 377-4800
All rights reserved.

Design by Roth Creative Services
Edited by Christine Hilt Muehlenberg

Printed in the United States of America
ISBN: 0-911493-22-0

Published In North America by:
BLUE SKY MARKETING INC.
PO Box 21583-S
St. Paul, MN 55121 USA
(651) 456-5602 / 800-444-5450
SAN 263-9394
8   7   6   5   4   3   2   1

Dedicated to Mrs. Claus,
The Elves, and
All of My "Helpers"

Foreword

I was Santa Claus. Seriously, for twelve years, I was Santa Claus. I'm not kidding, I really was!

I didn't intend to be Santa Claus. In fact, I didn't even want to be Santa Claus. "It just sort of happened."

This is a true story of a Christmas miracle that worked itself over a dozen years and countless moments of seasonal magic. It happened in a small town in the Midwest. And, of all things, it happened to me! How it happened and what happened is this book's story.

As you read it, you'll find yourself laughing and, perhaps, even crying. More importantly, you will assuredly find your spirits renewed and refreshed. And, when you're finished, you'll understand the truth of my statement.

Why it happened to me, I'll never know. But, that it happened is something for which I will be forever grateful.

So, come with me as I recall my journey and let me share the story with you, while there's still time to believe in Santa Claus!

Bob Litak

Prologue

When my secretary buzzed me on the intercom and told me that a lady from the Chamber of Commerce was on the phone, I had half a mind to dodge the call.

As an attorney starting up my own firm in a suburban setting of Milwaukee, I knew that making connections and contributing to the community were part of getting established. What I didn't want to get involved with were more fund raising activities that would stretch an already tight budget, made even tighter by the birth of our first child and the upcoming Christmas holidays.

Although running behind in my appointments, I took the call rather than risk offending the lady on the line or suggesting that my availability for civic projects was less than enthusiastic.

To my relief, the caller wasn't after money. It seemed that the Chamber's current project, "A Visit with Santa Claus," had run into a slight problem. No Santa! The gentleman slotted for the role had taken ill and wouldn't be available.

Apparently, my outgoing personality had again served me poorly and my name had been the unanimous choice to become the substitute Santa. Even though I tried weakly to get off the hook, claiming no prior employment experience, the caller's plaintive persistence and my need to get on with my workday moved me to accept the invitation. After all, how much difficulty could there be in putting on a red suit, repeating a few "Ho, Ho, Ho's," and announcing over and again "Merry Christmas?"

I can assure you that I had absolutely no ambition to do anything more than make a passable showing in the role, and then, only for the purpose of business development. The thought of giving up a precious Saturday after-noon so close to Christmas wasn't really high on my list of priorities. Perhaps the photo opportunity with my wife and new daughter might get the equation to balance.

As I quickly noted the appointment on my calendar and grabbed my briefcase to leave for court, I had no idea of the journey upon which I had embarked....

Cedarburg, Wisconsin, is a small town just outside of metropolitan Milwaukee. Historic buildings, mid-19th century architecture and a collection of unique mercantile establishments carrying out the town's turn of the century theme make it a most popular tourist destination, not only for the state, but for the Midwest and the country as a whole.

An active merchant's association, better known as the Chamber of Commerce, was constantly seeking new and better ways to drum up business and promote tourism.

Any resident of the town could testify to the Chamber's success after encountering the weekend and special festival traffic jams that would have been the envy of any LA rush hour.

But, if there was one time of year when the Chamber's efforts were nothing less than redundant, it was at Christmas. That's when the town truly sparkled. Just driving through it gave one a sense of emotional renewal. Cedarburg, at Christmas time, was picture perfect.

Wrought iron streetlights hung with garlanded decorations, strings of miniature white lights outlining every downtown building feature, and the old fashioned storefront displays all bespoke the beauty and magic of so many Christmases past. If you ever wanted to visit a life sized Currier and Ives setting, Cedarburg would be your destination.

But, even for those steeped in 19th century tradition, 20th century economics still played a large part in the town's personality. It was into this assemblage of seasonal offerings that the Chamber had invested.

Among the more prominent Yuletide events was an opportunity to let the town's young children visit with Santa Claus. Now, believe me, this was some kind of first class promotional effort. It was the kind of thing that a major retailer wouldn't dare try, because without the donated items and volunteer services, it wouldn't have had a very good effect on the bottom line. But, in Cedarburg, volunteerism and tradition were alive and well.

The Chamber's concept was simple. Take a large room off the Community Center/gym and convert it to look like the living room of Santa's home at the North Pole. Decorate it with "Claus-type" artifacts, add a Christmas tree with presents and line the walls with reindeer harnesses replete with shiny brass nametags. Include an old-fashioned pot-bellied stove, a fireplace mantle festooned with letters to Santa, and most important of all, a big throne-like chair in which the jolly old elf could hold court for the children.

When you topped all of that off with a little crass commercialism, by giving away free photos of the children with Santa, the malls and department stores were up against some pretty fierce competition.

It was into this setting that I naively walked, never realizing the changes it would have on my heart and soul....

Chapter 1

The doorbell at my home rang about mid-morning on the Saturday of my scheduled debut. I answered it and was confronted by a young lady with a badly fragmented cardboard box, which, she claimed, held everything I needed for my appearance later that afternoon as Santa.

Expressing my thanks for bringing it by the house, I wished her a Merry Christmas, and she wished me, "Good Luck!"

So, "It's out of brown boxes that Santa arises," I said to myself as I opened the package. Inside I found a rather well worn pair of oversized red pants with fake fur trim and no means of support. Was it possible my actual size had been incorrectly reported? Was I to be suited with what appeared to be slipcovers for the Goodyear blimp? No matter. My inspection of the equally natty coat that completed my ensemble left me convinced that stuffing was going to be needed.

As I examined a wide black belt that accompanied the costume, a chalky white parcel dropped to the floor. Upon closer inspection, I concluded it to contain my beard and hairpiece. Momentarily confused as to which was which, I finally managed to correctly identify each of the items and went to a mirror to try them on.

The vision that confronted me was not quite the effect I had hoped to portray. In fact, my dark mustache and eyebrows made it certain, in my mind, that I was about to ruin any number of young children's dreams by inadvertently exposing Santa as a fake.

With the appointed hour of my charade approaching, I decided that a quick trip to the cosmetic counter at the local pharmacy was definitely in order. Off I went, the brown box under my arm, and my pride on the line.

Discarding any thought of explaining my predicament to the lady behind the counter, I made a hasty selection from the lipstick, rouge and make-up displayed before me. It was from this assemblage of foreign chemicals that I hoped to emerge as a passable Santa.

On the short drive to the Community Center, my mind filled with thoughts and ideas about how I would portray Santa. None of my ideas appealed to me, and I was worried that they would appeal even less to the children I was about to meet. I decided to just try and get through make up and costuming and worry about what to say later. It was a little after noon and "Show Time" was at 1:00 P.M..

Arriving at the Community Center, I asked the building custodian, "Where does Santa change?" I don't know if the question took him by surprise or if he was simply stunned to find a grown man asking it, but I could see it had an unsettling effect on him. Regaining his composure, he pointed me towards a locker room—a girl's locker room!

After knocking rather loudly on the door, and secretly hoping to be turned away, I entered the locker room and, to my relief, found it empty. Placing the box containing the Santa suit on one of the long gray benches that paralleled the rows of lockers, I went to the bathroom mirror with my bag of cosmetics in hand. Standing there, I made ready to complete the transformation from mere mortal to Santa Claus, or at least how I thought he might look.

I applied some kind of white "goo" to my eyebrows and mustache, lightening them to an acceptable shade of gray. With an eyebrow pencil, I put some wrinkles on my forehead, around my eyes and down my cheeks. A little more pencil smeared here and there on my face passed for soot. Although the application wasn't as smooth as I'd hoped for, the overall impression was better than anticipated.

Placing the elastic support for the beard on the top of my head, I adjusted the whiskers to cover as much of my face as possible. Looking in the mirror, I was pleased with my effort. As I placed the wig on my head, I found the transition I had effected to be quite good—if I did say so myself.

Turning from the mirror, I was startled to find that I was not alone. Emerging from behind the far row of orange lockers was a lady whose dress and stature left no doubt that she was, and could only be, Mrs. Claus.

The first thing that struck me about her appearance was its perfection. The lady was as pleasantly short and round as one would expect Santa's mate to be. Her face was both youthful and full of wisdom; her eyes sparkled with enthusiasm and joy. Her attire consisted of a long white dress under a red and green apron trimmed with miniature candy canes. Covering her silver-gray hair was a red and white checkered bonnet accented with a sprig of holly. Her clothing was exactly what the well-dressed Mrs. Claus would wear throughout time.

Eyeing me through gold-rimmed granny glasses, she spoke, "You must be my new Santa Claus." The obviousness of her assessment was eclipsed by her unstated confidence in my ability to carry off the work. I found encouragement in her tone of voice. I had hope, that together, we might make a lot of children happy that day.

I introduced myself, taking great pains to make my ignorance of the role and what it entailed very clear to her. I learned her name was Anne, and that she had been Mrs. Claus for a number of years. She told me that, while she made hundreds of appearances, the visit with Santa in Cedarburg was her favorite. A feeling of apprehension at the possibility of single handedly changing her mind with my forthcoming performance came over me.

As she helped me into the pants and coat, Anne delivered an exhaustive list of "Santa Do's and Don'ts." It was quite obvious that I was in the presence of an expert in the field, and my mind raced to make mental notes.

Satisfied with the costuming effort, she marched me before the mirror and told me to put on my cap. "Carefully," she said, "It's the cap that makes the Santa!" As I put the cap on over the wig and whiskers, I witnessed a transformation that gave meaning to Anne's statement. "Hey, look. I'm Santa Claus. I really am!" She was absolutely right. It is the cap that makes the Santa.

Anne handed me a string of sleigh bells. *(From where they suddenly appeared, I'd never know.)* As we exited the locker room arm in arm, I tried to steal an inner moment of thought to prepare myself for my impending role.

That would be denied me. The door of the locker room opened directly to the visitor end of the Community Center's basketball court. We emerged just as the visitors were executing a fast break. As we stopped the play, I witnessed the effect that the appearance of Santa Claus can have on a crowd of people regardless of age, sex or present preoccupation.

The crowd broke into cheers and exclamations that would have been somewhat intimidating had I not immediately recognized that they were directed to Santa and not to me, who, after all, was only the guy in the suit. Any momentary embarrassment quickly faded and I slipped into my role and began dispensing the obligatory "Ho, Ho, Ho's " and "Merry Christmas" to my newly met fans.

Mrs. Claus and I proceeded down the court, which I ascertained to be sixteen "Ho's" and four "Merry Christmases" in length, before finally reaching the rear entrance to Santa's Room.

Entering the room, I found it to be a most impressive re-creation of that which would be immediately familiar to anyone even mildly acquainted with the story of Santa Claus and his North Pole home. Several of the Chamber volunteers introduced themselves to me and gave me a quick rundown on how the operation worked. I was told that, before the children came into the room, I'd receive a small slip of paper giving me their names in advance, hopefully in the same order in which they entered. *(So, that's how he did it.)*

A gentleman introduced himself as another Chamber member, who had volunteered to take the instant pictures. He gave me a few hints on how to position the children to get the best photos. My amateur status caused me to listen carefully and take his instructions most seriously.

Making a few last minute adjustments to my beard and costume, Anne escorted me to my chair and helped me get comfortable in it. She then assumed her traditional place of standing, beside her spouse, and signaled to the assembled multitude that Santa was ready to receive them.

I stole a quick glance out the door through which the children would enter the room. I concluded from the size of the waiting line that there could be very few youngsters under the age of 10 anywhere else in a five-state radius. What had I gotten myself into?

The next several hours passed in a successive blur of children *(of all ages, temperaments, manner of dress, and conversational ability)*, proud parents, and questions interrupted only by the momentary relief of the Polaroid's flash.

I soon learned that Santa was an extremely respected folk figure. He is endowed with knowledge that extends far beyond the season with which he is most identified. His powers and abilities are almost without limitation, and his word is the closest thing to scripture that will fall on the ears of those who share a belief in his existence.

I found myself rapidly aging in wisdom as I progressed through my on the job training, all the time receiving gentle guidance from Anne, or rather, Mrs. Claus.

I remember that, towards the end of the day, my wife arrived bringing our daughter for her first visit with Santa. We took several family portraits in order to take advantage of a photo opportunity that I did not intend to repeat. As I held my daughter in my arms and my wife sat on my knee, a feeling stirred deep within me that I couldn't identify. I felt myself drawn closer to the mystery and joys of the season than ever before. A sense of family, like none ever before, passed over me.

As the last child exited the room, I could see that it was already dark outside. The three-hour shift had stretched to nearly five. I guess no one has the heart to turn away a child waiting for

Santa, and I learned that the scheduled hours were only an estimate. As all in the room made ready to leave, I noticed Anne collecting the letters, drawings and lists the children had brought us that afternoon. She was carefully placing them in a large cloth folio for safe-keeping. The folio, well worn and obviously the property of Mrs. Claus, seemed especially appropriate to the irregularly sized and shaped papers and objects it so gently accepted. It struck me as a lovely gesture; such trusting childhood efforts should never be consigned to a trash receptacle.

As we exited the room and walked across the now empty and quiet gymnasium towards the locker room, a strange sense of satisfaction descended on me. I realized that the afternoon had been a learning experience like none other. I had been allowed to journey back to the memories of my youth and to see, from a magical perspective, that which makes the experience of childhood at Christmas so dear. Anne must have known what I was thinking as she broke the momentary silence and said, "Santa sees many things."

I was grateful for the experience, but equally glad that a long and hard day was over.

In the locker room, I quickly removed the wig and beard. I then took the suit off from over my street clothes, which I discovered to be thoroughly soaked with perspiration. *("What does he wear under his suit?" I asked myself.)* Moving to the sink and mirror, I set about removing my makeup. I noticed Anne putting on her coat to leave. "Not changing here?" I asked. "Oh no!" was her quick reply. "I've got three more appearances tonight and will be lucky to be home before 11:00."

I had to stop myself from asking aloud where this lady found the energy. Even more to the point, where did she find the time?

As we parted company on the steps outside of the building, Anne told me that she thought we really provided a great day for the children and parents who had visited with us. Her next comment stopped me cold. She told me that I was the best Santa she'd ever worked with, and she truly hoped we'd do it again. "Maybe sometime," I responded, more out of politeness than intent. " Maybe sometime...."

Walking across the now snow covered parking lot to my car, I noticed that Anne proceeded to get into a rather aged and not very reliable looking vehicle. Pleased to see her car start, and relieved that I wouldn't have to assist her in one of my least favorite winter rituals, I thought about how absolutely ordinary this lady was out of her lovingly crafted character of Mrs. Claus. Interesting....

I got into my car and allowed the contoured seats to offer me the physical relief denied by that big old wooden chair. The engine roared to life as I turned the key, and I started for home, hydration and the rest of my holiday season.

I saw through the windshield that an abundant number of stars seemed exceptionally bright and the night remarkably clear. A good night for "flying," I thought to myself—just the kind Santa would like.

P.S. In my heart I was glad that I had accepted the invitation to play Santa; it was the sort of thing everyone should try at least once!

Chapter 2

Nearly a year had passed and the altogether unexpected compliments paid me shortly after my stint as Santa had faded from memory.

You can imagine how surprised I was when I heard that it had been announced, at the November Chamber meeting, that I had again agreed to become the town Santa Claus. Okay. "Enough is enough," I said to myself. I set out to discover who had "volunteered" me and to correct their misguided thinking that I was interested in an annual role in the season's festivities.

It didn't take long to find out that the Chamber, in confirming Anne's return engagement, received a request from Anne herself that I reprise the role of her seasonal spouse. I knew it, I knew it, I knew it! I had been emotionally kidnapped. My immediate instincts were to abandon any idea of further participation right then and there. But, before I could even build myself a case to support my decision, the memories of that special afternoon and the feelings I came away with took control. There was no way I was going to refuse the request of this lady who gave so much and expected nothing in return.

I decided that, if I were going to donate the time and effort again, I would polish up the presentation a bit. Two things were definitely in order—improvement to my make up and to my apparel. A trip to a theatrical costume shop in Milwaukee yielded the required items. It also introduced me to an incredibly diverse assortment of Santa supplies. I remember that, as I looked them over, I found them interesting but, not to an extent that I would need to invest in other than a few basic essentials.

I purchased a selection of pre-packaged Santa makeup, some white gloves and boot sleeves. The last item I deemed to be essential as a result of my observation of the on-the-spot research done by children visiting Santa. Let me explain.

You may have noticed that children often direct their gaze in a downward direction when visiting with Santa. Since few adults ever have the opportunity to portray the jolly old elf, most of us take it for granted that this is a manifestation of shyness. Wrong, mistletoe breath! They're checking on Santa's boots, which to his young visitors, are the barometers by which the true Santa can be identified.

In my first effort, I simply put on some old dress boots. I noticed the children looking at them very, very carefully. It became quite obvious to me that the boots were an important part of Santa's overall image and that I had better get a child proof pair right away. My purchase of the boot sleeves turned my ordinary boots into the knee high and fur trimmed kind that were exactly what Santa was expected to wear. This technical adjustment served Santa's interests very well in re-enforcing his young visitors' acceptance of his physical existence.

The gloves that I purchased were to soften my hands, which are somewhat large, and perhaps a little too strong looking for a person as gentle as Santa.

In undertaking this analysis of Santa's personality and how it manifested itself in his apparel, I had begun to take the role a lot more seriously than intended. My focus was on how Santa would want to be seen by his youthful audience. I was concerned that the illusion I was trying to create was not as real as I could make it. Although I didn't realize it, in my heart, I had made an unconscious decision to become the best Santa the town had ever seen.

To keep my story from turning into a novel, I'm only going to relate one or two memories from each of the succeeding years of my role. This will also let me better share with you what Santa sees and hears from behind the beard and whiskers, and perhaps, what goes through his mind and heart.

I'll quickly tell you that the makeup and attire improved measurably during the second year. Also, I remembered to wear only gym shorts under the suit. That saved a lot on my physical well being, not to mention dry cleaning.

Although there are so many memories, two stand out from all the rest.

The first is of a lovely young girl who was mentally challenged. She met me for the first time with a rush to hug me that would have toppled me from my chair had not Mrs. Claus steadied it for me. Loving, trusting and outgoing in a manner without reservation, she was absolutely delightful. We would become the best of friends. No, wait. What am I saying? We were, from the moment our eyes met, the best of friends.

I told her that she was my special friend and in honor of that distinction I would share a Santa secret with her. I told her what Rudolph's favorite treat was. No, not sugar lumps. Not cookies either. Cake? You're getting colder. It's bubble gum! Don't believe it? You'd better. After all, would Santa lie to you? *(Oh, by the way, Rudolph isn't allowed to chew bubble gum while airborne—too much risk of popping a bubble over his nose and compromising our guidance system.)*

My second memory relates to understanding the true personality of Santa Claus. I came to learn that those who undertake to preserve it must come to terms with human shortcomings that would never bother the man in the red suit.

I recall, that year, a particular toy was incredibly popular. By virtue of the demand for it, it was practically unattainable. As you may have guessed, every other child's plea was for that toy. I looked to the parents each time I received the request, hoping for an affirmative nod. Each time, almost without exception, the response afforded me was a negative shake of the head. This situation contradicted Santa's ability to always bring that gift which would make his young visitors most happy. It had the potential to place Santa's "reality" in peril.

Now, you should understand that to be real, Santa has to be absolutely faithful to his image. If he fails in one respect, he's real in none. To make a promise to a child that might not be kept would destroy his reality. And, because Santa's the one person every child trusts completely, and to whom they commit their precious belief in the magic and mystery of the season, I came to understand the most important Santa rule ever— Santa never promises anything.

I learned, from that day on, to respond to each child's request, not with a promise to fulfill it, but to provide hope that it would be

answered in some way. I think there's
a lesson for all of us in that. I certainly
found one.

   *P.S. I added a second family portrait to my
collection. So did Anne.*

Chapter 3

By the time the next year rolled around, I was feeling pretty comfortable in my role and I readily acquiesced to Anne's gentle request that I work with her on the two Saturdays that immediately preceded Christmas that year. We were now two-thirds of the Chamber's promotion and had gained some local notoriety.

I suspect the local fame, which had begun to attach itself to our presentation, was due, in large part, to our real personalities having been completely taken over by our roles. Anne and I had developed a line of patter and interactive dialogue that delighted the children and entertained the adults who brought them. The only problem was, that Anne and I were having so much fun, we often found ourselves working late into the evening to the consternation of the other volunteers. And, that leads me to my memory of the third year.

After completing our parade down the gym floor, Anne and I entered our room and began chatting with the volunteers, who, except for the camera lady, were in universally high spirits. I remember speaking with her and asking, "Is anything wrong?"

"Wrong? Nothing's wrong except I'm not supposed to be here. If I hadn't been put on the spot by my boss, I'd be out doing my last minute shopping and not stuck here," she responded in an icy tone that was chilling even by North Poles standards.

In an effort to banish the negative aura she was injecting into my ordinarily felicitous domain, I told her that I understood her predicament and we'd get her a replacement in about an hour; she'd have the greater part of the afternoon to herself.

The afternoon flew by as usual, and our first break didn't come for almost two and one half-hours. I noticed that the camera lady was still with us. Fearing that her replacement had failed to show up, I cautiously approached her in hopes of at least expressing my personal thanks for staying with us.

"I'm sorry we intruded on your schedule this way," I said. "I really thought we had a replacement for you."

"Oh, you did; he was here about an hour or so ago. I sent him home," she responded.

"But, I thought you had some pressing personal matters to attend to. Frankly, I'm surprised to find you still here," Santa said.

"Surprised? You shouldn't be surprised. This is the best time I've had in years. If you and Mrs. Claus aren't perfect for this job, I'm the Easter Bunny," she replied to my complete amazement. "I wouldn't miss this show for the world; you two really are Santa and Mrs. Claus."

Knowing this lady was not the Easter Bunny *(with whom I am personally acquainted, and who looked nothing like her at all)*, it struck me that Anne and I had unknowingly touched an adult heart while reaching out to our young pilgrims. I told Anne what the camera lady said and why she would be staying with us to the end of the day. I wasn't as much puzzled by Anne's lack of surprise at the turn of events as I was by her knowing acceptance. Then it hit me. What Anne did so very well, I had somehow learned to do too. And, together, we had become a Yuletide force to be reckoned with....

P.S. Another family portrait and several more for Anne.

P.P.S. All children visiting Santa are not housebroken.

Chapter 4

To celebrate this year's anniversary together as Mr. and Mrs. Claus, I decided to let my hair down. Actually, I decided to throw it out all together and I once again found myself at the theatrical costumer intent on buying the very best hairpiece and beard they had to offer.

I picked out the most luxurious beard and wig I had ever seen. Silky, silver-gray strands of long wavy hair melted into a flowing white beard that gently descended almost to my waist. Imported and hand made, the price was a bit steep. Rather than disclose it to you, let's just say it's one of those pricey purchases that all who are married keep from their spouses. But, I was too heavily invested in Santa now to worry about that trifling issue. Besides, I knew Anne would love it.

I was like a child with a new toy that Saturday afternoon. I met Anne in the locker room and surprised her with our newest acquisition. I remember the joy and excitement we shared as Anne lovingly adjusted the wig and whiskers for me. I recognized that it was a reflection of the commitment that had grown between us to be the best Mr. and Mrs. Claus the town...no, the world, had ever seen!

That afternoon's performance was on the third Saturday of the season, and by the calendar, it was only a few days before Christmas. As a result of its scheduling, it was one of the busiest of any of our presentations to date.

For some unknown reason, we seemed to have more newborn visitors than on any previous day. I noticed that, after each photo was taken, Anne would take the infant into her arms. Then, as she lovingly cradled the child, we spoke of Christmas memories yet to be made with the new parents. A beautiful expression would come over her face at each of those moments as she held the infants near to her. It was, to my imagination, much the same as that which would have crossed the face of another Mother on that very first Christmas. Only the matrimonial bonds between Santa and Mrs. Claus allowed me to see that in Anne's eyes there was a tinge of sadness. I made a quick regretful note of it and moved on.

This year was to be especially memorable because Santa discovered that really good children have a twinkle in their eyes *(not unlike that which he has in his)*. Efforts to discern the twinkling, indicative of exceptionally good behavior, were a source of newfound joy and laughter that day and for all the visits in the years to come.

Looking for twinkling became an integral part of our repertoire and one we enjoyed immensely *(as did the Moms and Dads)*.

The smiles and laughter we were able to generate, as I carefully examined each child's eyes for an appropriate level of twinkling, produced, what I yet consider to be, the vintage of all of the photos we ever took. The facial expressions that a child will generate to convince Santa that they've been good, and that their eyes are twinkling, must be seen to be appreciated. But, the real beauty of the children's efforts lay in their unconditional belief in a spirit embracable only during that short and ever so precious period of life we call childhood.

We visited with nearly three hundred children that day and were again exhausted when we finally were allowed to slump against our lockers before going home. I noticed that Anne was changing into "civvies" and not leaving in costume, as was her usual practice. I casually inquired as to her plans out of uniform. Anne gave me a one word answer—"Rest." I was understandably glad for her. Anne nearly exhausted herself during the season, appearing wherever and whenever requested. My two Saturday afternoon contributions paled in comparison to her efforts. I felt, as I always did, impressed by the breadth of her charity.

I wished I had left it at that. But, the conversation continued. I learned that Anne had been finding herself to be more tired than usual and that she had been to see a doctor. "Nothing serious," she assured me.

In the parking lot behind the Community Center we talked briefly of the season, exchanged our Christmas wishes, and parted for another year.

P.S. *Best family photos to date.*

P.P.S. *Prancer is the second most favorite reindeer; and, yes, Santa does use the front door if there's no fireplace or chimney.*

Chapter 5

The next year's annual "Big Gig" alerted Anne and me to the fact that we had become a sort of local legend. Believe me, this was not our intention. In fact, we rather enjoyed our anonymity and had a lot of fun with it *(I'm getting ahead of myself)*. But, legends have a way of building upon themselves and this year must have been a boom year for legend construction.

I initially became aware of that fact when I made a stop at the local hardware store just before the first of my two upcoming Saturday performances.

The owner, who knew of my double identity, had been the volunteer photographer at the Saturday production the week before. *(Even though the Chamber sponsored visits on the three Saturdays before Christmas, I only appeared at the last two. Anne worked all three. But, I never considered her work on the first Saturday to be more than a tune-up for the real thing.)* I asked him how many children had visited the "set." The number given me was exceedingly low, not quite a hundred. I expressed a concern as to whether some change was in the air and that Santa might be losing his appeal.

"No worry about that," he said. He told me that for the last several weeks the Chamber had received numerous calls and requests for the dates on which the "real" Santa would be in attendance. He laughingly applauded my popularity and local fame. I took his warning of the impending mob scene with an outward display of good humor. But, inside, my heart was bursting with joy and satisfaction.

My fondest memory of this year relates to my anonymity and the fun I had with it. It occurred in two parts, the latter substantially after the season was long past.

To fully appreciate it, you'll need to know that I had now become rather proficient at making myself up as Santa. Even my secretary, who *(for the first and only time)* came to sit on my lap, remarked that she would never have recognized me. I truly had come to look the part.

Into Santa's room this year came a delightful young child followed by his father, whom I immediately recognized as one of my most ardent professional adversaries and antagonists. *(Remember my "part time" job, when I wasn't Santa, was a lawyer.)* Now, Santa loves all children, regardless of any accident of birth. To reinforce that fact, I went out of my way to spend time and effort getting to know this particular child and make him comfortable with his red suited friend. As he departed the room, I called out to him and told him that if I didn't bring everything he wanted, he was to ask his dad to get it because he was a famous lawyer and could do anything. The look on my colleague's face was worth a thousand reindeer, perhaps two thousand. He was absolutely taken aback and completely mystified as to who I really was. He mouthed the inquiry, "Who are you?" to me.

"Santa," was my only response.

Several months would pass before the phone rang at my office and I found my formerly puzzled brother lawyer on the line. He hadn't called on business; no, he was calling to confirm the ugly rumor that I was Cedarburg's secret Santa Claus. I admitted that, through the workings of some unknown force, I had developed the ability to portray Santa. A mile wide smile crept over my face as he recounted the visit that had so puzzled him. He voiced his utter disbelief that I could step out of character and assume so well the role of a lovable and warm-hearted Santa. Then, he closed the call with an expression of his sincere thanks for the time that I spent with his son. I don't recall him ever acknowledging that conversation again as our professional paths crossed over the years. However, I did notice that he never scheduled anything with me in December.

In some ways, five years is a long time. In other ways, it's an exceedingly brief period, especially when you consider that Anne and I only existed for two days a year. That fact made the friendships we established with our young visitors and their families of even greater importance to us. Quite often a child's first visit to Santa might not occur until he or she was 4 or 5. If the myth could be preserved for a few short years, we realized that we should not expect to see our young friends much past the age of 9 or

10. Each time Anne and I visited with an older child we knew that this might be our last meeting. We wondered if, in the next twelve months, they would cross the threshold that separated us from those who had already moved ever so much closer to adulthood.

One notable exception to our concern was a lovely family of six children. They would visit us at nearly the last moment on the Saturday just before Christmas. The children all shared their mother's red hair and their father's tall lanky frame. At the time of their first visit, I guessed that the youngest was four and the oldest ten. They always wore their dress clothes, which were either a green plaid or stripe. These provided a lovely contrast to their auburn hair and freckled faces. This family came year after year, always on the same date and time, and neither Anne nor I would call it a day until we knew that our annual visit had been completed. Perhaps the most magical part of their appearance was the sense of renewal with which we began each visit. It was almost as if the twelve months separating our last meeting were mere seconds, and that these brief encounters were, in reality, nothing less than a continuation of a family's socializing with their northern-most relations. As the years passed, it was marvelous to watch the older children, who by then had progressed into young adulthood, participate in the visit to the benefit of the youngest in the group. I'm sure their parents were as delighted as Anne and I to see a family embrace each other in what had become a tradition. Neither Anne nor I ever learned the name of this family. Perhaps it was better that way. To have concluded our yearly visit and to later somehow learn, during the off-season, that it would not be repeated, would surely have broken our hearts.

At the end of that last Saturday's session I shared with Anne a "present" I had received earlier in the year. My wife and older daughter came by for our family portrait and brought with them our new daughter, Christine, age three months. As was her custom, following the photograph, Anne cradled Christine in her arms with the same love and affection she bestowed upon every other child she so held on each and every Saturday we had been together. There would be no special attention given my daughter. Mrs. Claus had no favorite children. She loved them all and she loved them equally.

In the locker room before I left for home that night, Anne confided in me that she was unable to have children of her own. I sensed that this was extremely difficult for her to accept. I felt saddened and could offer nothing more than my own inept expression of sympathy and understanding.

Oh how I wished I really *was* Santa....

P.S. Almost four hundred children today; best family portraits to date.

P.P.S. We're having an impact on the community; many of our visitors now know Rudolph's favorite treat is bubble gum.

Chapter 6

By the sixth year of our "reign" Anne and I had honed our roles to near perfection. We were even beginning to draw an audience some distance from Cedarburg. I learned that for a fact, one day, while in Milwaukee.

I had stopped at a large downtown mall and, from a second floor railing, was watching a mall santa *(I did not capitalize the "S" intentionally.)* to see how others might view the role. Two ladies standing next to me were talking about the lavish decorations surrounding the setting into which the mall had placed their version of St. Nick. *(No matter how hard I try, I just can't call someone else Santa.)*

"Scenery and decorations are nice," said one of the ladies. "But, if you want to have the Santa Claus experience of your life, go out to Cedarburg. They've got a Mr. and Mrs. Claus there who are absolutely fantastic! I've gone back twice; they're that real."

Could it be? Had our fame spread to the big city? Apparently so. When I met Anne in the locker room on Saturday, I told her about the conversation I had overheard. Anne smiled knowingly with a hint of satisfaction that her charitable heart would never allow her lips to speak.

Perhaps my fondest memory of this particular Christmas was of an event that partially related to my daughter, Jackie, who was now seven and very much into the Santa Scene. You can imagine how solidly integrated Santa was within our own household and the store of knowledge he possessed about my daughter's activities and those of her playmates. *(Over the years, this was a constant source of amazement and mystery to both of my daughters.)*

One of my daughter's best friends was a lovely little girl named Julia, who lived only a few houses down the street. She was exceedingly intelligent, to a degree that I sometimes thought as overshadowing her childhood innocence.

Her mother called our home the evening before the Saturday afternoon on which Julia was to visit Santa. She spoke with my wife about her concern that her daughter had figured out the Santa story prematurely. When I heard this, I immediately resolved to set the record straight that very next afternoon. Santa can't afford to allow any acceleration in the surrender of childhood innocence. Neither can the world.

About an hour into the next day's session, Julia came to sit on my knee. I could tell by the look on her face that there was suspicion in the air. Rather than adopt a defensive mode, I went straight to offense. "My elves tell me there's a rumor going around school that you're not sure if I'm real," I said. Julia looked up at me with a startled expression. "Now, see here young lady," I continued, "There are enough negative thoughts in this world without one of my special friends going around telling people that I don't exist." The child's look of astonishment intensified.

I then took Julia's hand and placed it at the tip of my beard. I challenged her to pull on it to see if it would come off. She could not observe that, with my other hand, I had grabbed the upper portion of the strand in such a way that she could tug against it for all time without effect. *(This was a valuable piece of "sleight of hand" that, once discovered, I would put to frequent and satisfying use in the years to come.)*

41

I next took her hand and placed it against my stomach, which I was pushing forward with all my might. "Now, does this feel like a pillow? Do you think I'm not really inside this suit?" I asked sternly. *(Or at least as sternly as Santa can say anything while laughing.)*

I asked Julia if she had recently played with her friend, Jackie. Suddenly speechless, she could only nod affirmatively. "I hope you two weren't chasing the ducks on the pond again," I said. "They're very good friends of the reindeer, and the elves won't like it one bit." A wide-eyed look of amazement came over Julia's face. I knew she was thinking, "How could he possibly know that?" I went on to talk about things that only one who knew her and her friends well would know. I only stopped when I was satisfied that she was thoroughly mystified, but more importantly, convinced of Santa's existence.

That evening her mother called and told me about the wondrous effect of the afternoon's visit. She was delighted that one of childhood's greatest joys had been preserved for her daughter. She jokingly reported that I had done such a good job, Julia might believe in Santa until she turned twenty-one!

I told her I hoped her daughter would believe in Santa for much longer than that. "I know what you mean," she said. We wished each other a Merry Christmas and I put the phone down ever so gently.

This year Anne and I also developed a process to speed up our assembly line.

It should be understood that for all the preparation that a child goes through to visit Santa, the actual confrontation is sometimes overwhelming. It can frequently leave even the most verbal and enthusiastic child speechless.

When children come to talk with Santa, it's usually about that most important gift. Frequently, when I asked, "What is it you're hoping Santa will bring you for Christmas?" a child would adopt a stone-faced silence. I quickly learned that the longer I waited for an answer, the less likely it was that I would receive one. This necessitated my invention of "The

Surprise." "The Surprise" was a special gift, offered in response to a child's momentary monastic vow of silence. It invariably produced a positive utterance or, at the very least, a nodding of the head. That would be enough to let Santa and his guest off their holiday hook. The parents most assuredly understood what "The Surprise" would be. *(The child had talked their ears off about it for months before coming to see Santa.)* I knew they would make certain that the tag on the special present read "From Santa."

When you're seeing children by the hundreds, a few minutes saved here and there can add up to a lot more quality time with those who really want to participate in their visit.

(Oh, by the way, Mrs. Claus and I always made sure to remind the children that "The Surprise" would be wrapped in "Red and Green" paper, not green and red, because that was the ordinary kind of paper that the stores sold, and it wasn't special. Ours was special because it was "Red and Green." You probably wouldn't be able to tell the difference yourself, but the children could.)

Chapter 7

Seven years had now turned our Mr. and Mrs. Claus into seasoned as well as seasonal personalities. I remember that year well because of a compliment we received from a most unexpected source.

A well-dressed stranger had been in the room for the early part of the first Saturday session. At the break, this gentleman approached me and introduced himself. He was a theatrical agent from New York City and represented a major production company. He expressed his appreciation for the roles Anne and I had crafted and inquired as to whether or not we might like to expand on our performance. Needless to say, I was taken aback by his statement, let alone his awareness of our existence. I excused myself to speak with Anne, knowing full well that neither of us would have an interest in such an offer, but wanting to present a united front. Anne's response mirrored mine. We returned to the gentleman to thank him for his offer and to tell him how much we appreciated the compliment it represented. We knew, and he knew, our hearts were in Cedarburg. To do what we did for other than pure love and the enjoyment of sharing the joys of the season would have reduced us to mere actors. The gentleman was extremely polite in accepting our rejection of his proposal. I remember his parting words, "In watching you with the children, I knew before hand what your answers would be." Anne and I were glad it showed.

This year brought the youngest visitor we were ever to meet. A lovely young couple came in with their parents and a most special "present," a newborn baby girl, age two days.

I can't remember ever having been as nervous as when they placed the infant into my arms for the photo. Relief came none too soon, as Anne took the child from me after the camera's flash. As was her custom, Anne spoke lovingly to the new parents of Christmases yet to come. I had heard these words before; but, this time there was something different in Anne's tone of voice. I attributed it to the moment and the startling youth of this tiniest of visitors.

This was also the year my older daughter became embarrassingly insistent that I take her to see Santa. She continually reminded me about how, for one reason or another, I was never able to go with her or her sister. She told me that Santa was a special friend of hers. I asked her how she knew that, and she reported that he always said, "Ho, Ho, Ho! Well, if it isn't my old friend, Jackie," each time she entered the room. I mentioned that maybe Santa said that to all the children. "No! He told me that he only says that to me because I'm one of his special friends," she announced proudly. "I see," I said. "I don't blame him for that; you're very special to me too." And, having momentarily changed the subject, I let my perennial and predictable inability to visit Santa slip from the conversation. Jackie didn't pick up on it and I escaped from participation in visiting Santa for another year. I looked forward with mixed emotions to the day when Jackie and her sister, Christine, would learn that the family photos with Santa, were in reality, family photos of Santa.

P.S. *It's getting harder to hide my identity from Jackie (make a note to use more make-up remover); the photos are getting better every year; Anne and I really love this job!*

Chapter 8

As I opened the old brown box with my "work clothes" in it a few days before the second Saturday of December, I looked down at the cap that had come with the original outfit. It seemed to me that Anne and I had grown in our roles to a point where the cap was somehow now insufficient in character. Don't ask me to explain what it was that I found missing; I can't. But, I kept remembering what Anne said about it being "the cap that makes the Santa." Something moved me and I found myself once again at the theatrical costume shop considering several styles of Santa caps.

After a prolonged period of careful and exhaustive consideration, I found one that was just right. Big and luxurious, with red and white fur, it most definitely had a personality of its own. I took it home with me, bursting with anticipation and eager to show it to Anne.

In the locker room, I surprised Anne with the new cap. She carefully examined it and pronounced it to be "Perfect!" I asked her to place it on my head. As she did so, we gazed into the mirror and our annual transformation was renewed. Try as we might, peering into the mirror, we could not find our own reflections. We saw only Mr. and Mrs. Claus.

That year, due to some increased publicity, we had an even larger number of young visitors. Because we were doing this for the love of the experience, we spent as much time as was needed to assure each child that their visit would be neither hurried nor incomplete. Anne and I prided ourselves on this effort and I believe it was truly appreciated by the children and, perhaps, even more so by their parents. I know it distinguished us from the imposters at the malls and department stores.

This year would provide a memory not at all as pleasant as I would like to recall but with a lesson that could not be overlooked.

For those not familiar with the demographics of Cedarburg, Wisconsin, I should tell you that it's located in a prosperous, upscale and economically thriving area of the state. Perhaps that's why my first face to face confrontation with the poverty of a child stands out so clearly in my mind.

Over the years, as children entered the room, Anne developed an uncanny ability to tell me who they were and what was happening in their lives. How she did this I never knew. I suspected it was distilled from her involvement in numerous community activities, both seasonal and otherwise. Still, she had so much information....

On this Saturday afternoon, a little girl about six years old came in with her parents. From the cut and condition of their clothing, I could see that this family was existing on a much lower economic level than any Santa had previously encountered. Anne confirmed this, whispering into my ear that she knew them and that hard times would not allow for any presents for the little girl this year. I couldn't believe it, and whispered back something to challenge that fact. Anne repeated her statement, again advising me to avoid the subject of a present altogether.

I must tell you that this was the most difficult visit I had ever participated in with any child. How do you tell a little one that, amidst all the decorations and presents on display, there is not one for her? My heart screamed at my conscience. I felt all of society's pains suddenly descend on me. For the first time ever, Santa was angry. Then, as if it could get no worse, I foolishly asked the child what she would like most for Christmas. Her two-word answer haunts me to this day. "Anything new."

What could I say or do? I was trapped there in my chair and confined in that costume. Separated by circumstance from any personal ability to right this incredibly unfair wrong, I prayed for insight. Perhaps that prayer was heard, for somehow it came to me to gently tell the little girl that of all the things in life that are new, that which we treasure most would be a new friend. I told her that Mrs. Claus and I would put forth our best efforts to see to it that she would soon meet a new friend. I assured her that this friendship would provide more joyous times than anything we could wrap in our special "Red and Green" paper. It must have worked because her face broke into a smile so very wide and she gave me a hug "for all time." As she left the room, I brushed my whiskers slightly upwards, hoping to hide a tear.

But, this year also brings memories of some of our best comedic episodes as well. Two come quickly to mind.

The first, resulted from a visit by a group of cheerleaders. These young ladies, older and already acquainted with Santa Claus, engaged in good-natured fun and some memorable photos while seated on Santa's lap *(with a suitably disapproving Mrs. Claus looking on)*. In answer to my traditional question as to what they wanted for Christmas, I suggested "a boyfriend for each day of the week." That met with a torrent of teenage giggles and laughter only surpassed in volume when I added, "That probably wouldn't work out, because they'd be too difficult to get into the sack." And with that line, we came about as close as we ever did to losing our "G" rating!

The second, relates to a bit of improvisation created to deal with the occasional child whose behavior might have left room for improvement. Anne and I found that threatening to leave a "Purple Hippopotamus" in their room on Christmas morning, for the child to clean up after, usually produced a torrent of ardent promises of better behavior. Now, you probably wouldn't be threatened by the possibility of awakening on Christmas to find a "Purple

Hippopotamus" sharing your bedroom. But, then again, you probably don't believe that reindeer can fly!

In the locker room that evening, Anne confided in me that she wasn't feeling well and that she had some continuing concerns about her health. I asked if there was anything I could do and she said, "Just being able to tell you is enough."

I told her that my Christmas wish for her this year would be better health and abundant happiness. I reminded her that Santa's requests, when received by the Infant, were believed to merit special attention. She smiled appreciatively, and I kissed her gently on her cheek. It was wet with a tear.

P.S. Better photos than last year; Rudolph continued in his string of unbroken victories as the most popular of the reindeer; Mrs. Claus is insisting that the children leave me low fat milk and cookies. I suspect it has something to do with the "narrow chimneys" I have recently begun to encounter.

Chapter 9

My tenth year in the business created somewhat of a problem for my wife and I regarding our daughter, Jackie. It seemed that, because of the focus on Santa in our home around the holidays and the incredible knowledge he had about her, Jackie was steadfast in her belief as to his existence. Regardless of how lovely her belief was, there is a time in life when reality demands the truth be known and this was to be the year for Jackie.

After numerous attempts to approach the subject at home, necessarily out of hearing of her younger sister, I decided that I would talk with Jackie as we drove to a store. I told Jackie the truth about her visits with Santa. Her rejection of that unwanted information was, as you may have anticipated, somewhat more adamant than would be expected from another child. Add to this already trying circumstance the fact that your dad's also telling you he's

Santa, and you have the makings of an emotional volcano.

"You couldn't be Santa," Jackie told me. "You don't even sound like him." In an effort to prove my point, I repeated Santa's greeting to Jackie in my normal voice. "See dad, that's not how Santa sounds," she said, both self-satisfied and relieved. Then, I lowered my voice to that which Santa used. I repeated the greeting. Jackie nearly froze on the spot. "Dad, you sound just like Santa!" And, with that pronouncement, she crossed the threshold to adulthood that Santa so dislikes.

I told her that the store we were going to was actually the theatrical costume shop and that I was going to purchase some Santa spectacles *(in as much as I had aged significantly in the last few minutes)*. At the same time, we were going to get her an elf costume. I was not going to break up a great act. "I'm going to be my dad's, no, I mean Santa's elf," she said. As she spoke those words, the anguish we had both experienced moments before was forgotten. We drove to the costume shop with our hearts once again wrapped in special "Red and Green" paper.

I had already spent an hour making up Jackie that Saturday when Anne met our new recruit. To say it was love at first sight would have been an understatement. Anne took to Jackie as if she were her very own elf. *(After all, isn't Mrs. Claus mother to all of the elves?)*

Anne and I gave Jackie some last minute instructions on "Elfdom" *(Or, is it "Elfism?")* and how she should act. She took them to heart and her performance that day was incredible, if I say so myself. Her presence brought fresh vitality to the act and gave our visitors, both young and old, something new and joyful to see. *(After witnessing her performance that day, I still think that elf must have had some Santa in her.)*

To explain the presence of one of the North Pole's finest citizens, Anne and I declared that our elf had won the "Candy Cane Painting Contest." Because of this elf's demonstrated ability to paint the straightest stripes on the candy canes we gave away, this particular elf was invited to accompany us to Cedarburg. We had more fun with that story and its variations than I can relate. I don't think our guests ever tired of hearing it. *(To this day, I am exceedingly critical about the straightness of the stripes on candy canes.)*

I recall that year we also began to spread the word that Santa was using the airspace over Cedarburg for practice flights with the reindeer and sleigh. We began to tell the children that if they looked up in the sky on a clear night they might see the lights on the reindeer harnesses and Rudolph's red nose flashing. Santa was pleased to hear many of the children tell of having seen the lights. *(I silently thanked every pilot who flew over Cedarburg on those particular nights for unknowingly helping us out!)*

I noticed with some concern that we had to take a few more, and somewhat extended, breaks that year. Anne seemed more tired than usual, although it never showed when children were in the room. I was worried about her health; after all she was my "wife."

That year we finally decided to surrender our anonymity. A sign was placed above the entrance to Santa's room proclaiming that Anne and I *(using our real names)* had "donated the air fare" to fly Mr. and Mrs. Claus to Cedarburg. This contrivance allowed for our adult visitors to learn our true identities, while the children thought little or nothing of the advertisement. People who knew either of us always commented on how unrecognizable we were in our roles and make-up. That didn't seem at all strange to either of us, who were, for a few hours on each of those joyous Saturday after-noons, Santa and Mrs. Claus. Never mind what the sign said.

In the locker room that evening, as Anne and I changed into our street clothes, we spoke of the fact that this was a special anniversary for us. Ten years and still a very happily married Mr. and Mrs. S. Claus. Our thoughts turned to the older children and young adults we had met over the years and what had become of them. Some might now be parents themselves. Had the "gifts" we shared with them been enough to make them want to preserve the magic of our myth for their children? We hoped so with our hearts and souls.

I reluctantly asked Anne about her health. Her answer was in line with my observation of her loss of energy and change in physical appearance. I learned that her illness was very serious. I was completely incapable of any understanding as to why such a good and kind person as my seasonal spouse should be so afflicted.

Could not the wonders of the season be increased in number to include a cure for Anne? Was a prayer for relief too much to ask?

I thought Christmas was supposed to be a time for miracles. Where then was Anne's miracle? I could think of no person who deserved one more. She had worked thousands for others.

P.S. For the first time since I took this job, I'm a little weary of it. In my heart, I'm worried about Anne and I not being together again next year. The pictures we took have a very special and very different meaning this year.

Chapter 10

As I entered the locker room for the eleventh year, I was thrilled to see Anne already there, looking better than ever, and in great spirits. She told me that she was feeling much better and had new hopes of beating the threat posed by her illness.

I told her that her news was the best Christmas present I could receive.

We spoke of the crowds we were generating and of the fun we had now that our roles had been inextricably woven into our personalities.

I commented that, with time, the stuffing in my suit wasn't as necessary as it once was and that I had started to fill the suit out on my own. Anne assured me that I was every bit as handsome as when she first met me some four or five centuries ago.

My memories of this year, which unbeknownst to me would be the next to last, are rather general. Maybe that's because Anne and

I had perfected our repertoire to a point where we enjoyed the afternoon more than anyone else in attendance.

To that end, we conducted "The Most Popular Reindeer Contest," with the perennial and undisputed champion, Rudolph, emerging victorious.

We threatened to leave our infamous "Purple Hippo," negotiated for "Surprises" and recounted how our elf helper had won the "Candy Cane Painting Contest" and with it the prized trip to Cedarburg. We did all this to the great delight of the children and even more apparent enjoyment of their parents, relatives and friends.

We reminded children to watch the evening sky for our practice runs and the flashing lights on the sleigh and Rudolphs' red nose.

We accepted lists and letters, lovingly drawn crayon portraits of ourselves, and assured children who had moved from their last year's residence that Santa knew their new addresses. We made countless Moms and Dads happy by extracting promises of better behavior from their children over the holiday season.

I detected appropriate levels of twinkling and cautioned my young visitors about behavior that created lop-sided twinkling. We demanded "reindeer-wide" smiles from all of the children as they had their photos taken.

With the exception of one personal aside, which I'll share with you in a moment, what I remember most about our eleventh year in service was how routinely it went. Most amazing of all was that Anne and I still found it to be every bit as much fun, and as personally exhilarating, as our first time together. Ours had become a quality performance and we believed that things of quality had no fear of time.

My recollection of this year is particularly personal. It relates to a comment made by my daughter, Christine, at dinner, after she had visited Santa earlier that day. She was recounting her meeting and what she and Santa had talked about in great detail. I maintained an exaggerated level of interest even though I was watching on "instant replay." As I listened, I heard my emotional clock strike the eleventh hour, when she announced that, "Santa's elf looked a lot like Jackie!" Jackie laughed nervously to distract her sister from pursuing the comment. My wife and I looked at each other knowingly. I began to visualize the outfit my newest elf would wear next year.

P.S. The satisfaction I have derived from portraying my alter ego is my most cherished feeling this holiday season. It truly is in giving that we receive, and the gift I had received was beyond measure.

Chapter 11

As expected, I found it necessary to explain the whole Santa show to my younger daughter, Christine, some months before Christmas. It wasn't easy on me. Christine was even better prepared to debate the truth of my revelation than her sister before her.

I told her that she would be my new elf, and would, as her sister had, see the magic of the season from a perspective few are ever afforded. She agreed to participate, not so much in grudging acceptance, but more out of a curiosity to see to what extreme her dad would take this ridiculous charade about being Santa.

The delight with which I looked forward to my younger daughter's entry into her new role was enough to balance my disappointment in finding that my older daughter had truly outgrown her's. *(There's a little known rule at the North Pole—elves may not exceed 48 inches in height.)* This year's family portrait would be different. No one in the photo would be visiting with Santa. It would be a true family photo, and one that I had both looked forward to and had hoped to postpone.

Negative feelings ran high when I learned that Anne was too ill to participate in the first of our two Saturday performances. I called to speak with her and she assured me that her absence was due only to a "flu bug" and she'd shake it by the next Saturday. Making her promise to get better on "crossed candy canes," I told her about our newest cast member and how we were both looking forward to being together with her.

After making up Christine to a degree where she didn't even recognize herself, I set about performing my own, now familiar, metamorphosis. Christine watched intently as each item of Santa's apparel made its way onto my frame. She found the make up interesting, although not to the point of convincing her of my true identity. When I had completed dressing, and with wig and whiskers in place, I turned to face the mirror. Christine looked into the mirror with me as I placed the cap on my head. The expression that came over her face was one of complete astonishment. Dad was Santa! It was a moment forever etched in my heart. I told her quite solemnly that it was "all in the cap," just as Anne had told me years before.

That afternoon my elf and I put on a creditable showing. We particularly enjoyed interacting with many of Christine's unknowing friends and their younger brothers and sisters. It was a difficult performance, however, and I missed Anne's presence and the support she offered Santa. Most of all, I missed the support she provided me.

I felt that, even as hard as I had tried to fly on one wing, I hadn't quite pulled it off. The volunteers seemed to sense my frustration and were exceptionally supportive and helpful. I appreciated their efforts and those of my elf. It didn't help.

I was very glad to hear from Anne later that week and to learn that she'd be there on Saturday as promised. Christine and I got to the locker room early to make sure our make-up was in perfect order. I wanted Anne to get a great first impression of our new elf.

Anne came in and, true to her warm and loving nature, took to Christine like a long lost child. She dutifully examined my daughter's costume and make up, welcoming her to our "family" and pronouncing her "the best elf ever."

We were together at last! We were a family again. Out of the locker room we stepped. And, once more, to the cheers of the crowd, we stopped the ongoing basketball game. *(I think I even shot, and made, a free throw!)* As we ceremoniously marched the familiar route to Santa's room, my heart soared in expectation of a great afternoon.

As I entered the room, I saw within it the ugliest piece of furniture I had ever seen in my life. It was a second chair placed next to Santa's. Anne always stood next to Santa; there had never been a need for a second chair. I immediately knew it foretold of a progression in Anne's illness. I took that as a personal threat to Santa.

Amazingly, that afternoon was the most incredible performance Anne or I ever gave. The children and their parents were the most gracious and loving we could remember. Everyone we had hoped to see again returned and our most cherished friendships were renewed. We could do no wrong that day; every line, every joke, every action was perfection. Even the photos were the best ever taken.

My wife, Sherry, and my "retired elf," Jackie, came by later that afternoon for our family photo. We all clustered around Anne as we laughed and joked about how much our "family" had grown during our short twelve years together. The line of waiting children grew in length as we celebrated our love affair with the season and our roles in it. Only the reality of the hour and the knowledge that we were postponing the inevitable caused us to end our reunion.

Sherry and Jackie watched as Anne, Christine and I returned to visiting with the children. Sherry later told me that the scene was extraordinarily touching to her in a way she had never before felt. I knew what she meant.

At the end of the day, a delegation from the Chamber of Commerce came in and presented Anne with a gorgeous crystal figurine of "Santa In His Sleigh." She accepted it with a quiet dignity that bespoke her humility as one who would never openly acknowledge the joy she brought to so many children of all ages. With tears in her eyes, Anne turned to show the piece to me and I broke my most important Santa rule. Santa promised something. I promised her I would remember the moment forever.

To my recollection, that was the first, last and only promise Santa ever made.

The locker room was quiet as I changed out of uniform. The long gray benches seemed to accentuate the chill in the room. I was glad to see that Anne wasn't changing. I waited for her to inform me as to where she was off to that evening and to whom she would further extend the love and generosity of Mrs. Claus.

My heart broke as she told me of having learned from her physician that this could well be her last Christmas. Her illness had worsened and she was worried that her time on earth might now be measured in months. She told me that she wanted to leave tonight, dressed as she had been when we first met, so I would remember her that way. I told her that would never be possible for she had grown so much more beautiful to me during our years together. She smiled that famous knowing smile of hers, turned and walked out into one of the most beautiful moonlit and snow filled evenings I could ever remember.

I drove home in a silence unbroken by my daughter's respect, if not complete under-standing, for the tears on my cheeks.

P.S. The family pictures were, without doubt, the absolute best we had ever taken. We took many extras. They became immediate heirlooms of the heart.

Chapter 12

It was an early April morning that found me up at about 6 A.M. looking over some paper work and absent-mindedly listening to the radio. A traffic bulletin reporting a fatal automobile collision caught my attention. Perhaps it was because the intersection at which it had occurred was close to my office and one I considered as being very safe. I took comfort in knowing that none of the office staff were likely to be in the area at that hour. In fact, none were probably even awake yet.

That afternoon I made it a point to drive to the intersection where the morning's accident had occurred. I was drawn there without a conscious reason. As I passed through the intersection, I noted that it appeared exceptionally benign for what must certainly have been a tragic scene some hours prior. Still not understanding why I found

myself there, I gave the whole thing an
emotional shrug of the shoulders and went
back to the office, finished the day, and left
for home.

It was about 7:00 that evening when the
phone rang and I found the Chamber President
on the line. "Bob, has anyone called you about
Anne?" he asked. "No," was my terse answer, and
before he could speak further I asked if she had
passed away. "Yes, I'm sorry to tell you she has,"
he continued. "But, it wasn't her illness," he said.
"Anne died in an auto accident this morning."
Before he could speak another word, I identified
the intersection for him. He expressed his confu-
sion with my prior statement indicating a lack of
knowledge about Anne.

There was no way I could explain it to him.
I didn't even understand it myself. I thanked
him for the courtesy of his call and begged to
get off the line. I knew I needed time to think
about what I had experienced that day. I also
knew I must keep the news from my elves for at
least twenty-four hours. I was not going to spoil

a surprise party they had so carefully planned for the next day. Somehow, I would allow myself to be taken unaware and outwardly "celebrate" my birthday.

I remained in the very rear of the church at the funeral, absolutely intent on being unseen. I departed so quickly at the conclusion of the service that weeks later several people asked if I had even been there.

I found myself at mid-afternoon, on the last Saturday before Christmas that year, at Anne's gravesite. The simple headstone reflected nothing of the great joy and love the gracious lady it remembered had dispensed during her all too brief life.

Standing there I knew, in Santa's room at the Community Center, at that moment, children were visiting with a solitary Santa and Christmas memories were being made. I also knew that I had been given something very special and which I would forever consider my own personal Christmas miracle.

My thoughts were interrupted by my remembrance of the task at hand. I reached inside my coat and took out my Santa cap to lay it gently atop Anne's headstone. A silent prayer winged its way to the Infant, who I knew now held Anne in His arms. I turned and walked back to my car.

I don't know whether it was the biting wind or my emotions that brought the tears to my eyes. I do know that my thoughts flashed back to a very busy Saturday afternoon not so very long ago when, in a room filled with people, Anne and I spoke at length with a most delightful little girl and her mother....

I remembered asking the little girl if she had seen any elf footprints in the snow around her house. To my delight she answered, "Yes." I knew immediately that either her mom or dad shared the secret of making such footprints. (These are created by first placing the fleshy part of a fist onto a snow or frost covered surface and then touching the fingertips above the imprint. Alternating the procedure with one's left and right hands will leave a remarkably real set of imprints resembling small elfin feet.)

I asked her mother if she ever wondered, "Why do elves leave footprints when, as can be seen from our own elf's attire, they wear boots?"

"I really couldn't tell you, Santa," was her reply. "Why do they?"

I thought to myself, "All right, Santa. Why do they?"

I had painted myself into a Christmas corner. I had absolutely no idea as to why elves wore boots and left footprints. The room hushed. It seemed as though the whole world was waiting for my answer....

I listened to myself with an almost distant detachment as I said,

"Most people don't know that many of the homes the elves and I visited on our first Christmas Eve were of extremely poor families. We had not expected our gifts and toys to be amongst the things least needed by so many of the children we met. Their real needs were for food, shelter, and clothing.

Frequently, the children did not even have shoes for their feet to protect against the cold and snow.

This made the elves very sad. In turn, they began to leave their own boots for the children while they continued that night's long journey in bare feet. In the morning, their footprints spoke silently of the past evening's charity.

A remembrance of the elves' kindness and generosity has come down to us through the ages; for today, although elves may walk through the snow in boots, they will leave footprints."

I said no more.

At that moment, the fit of my suit was more natural and comfortable than ever before. I could not feel the adhesive of the whiskers nor the elastic straps for my beard; the wig felt as though it had become my own hair. I didn't know if the heat of the room was having an effect on me or if some other force was at work. I simply sat there in silent wonderment.

How had I come to know the words of a story that had never before been spoken?

"Santa, I thought I'd heard all of the

Christmas stories ever told, but I've never heard that one," the mother said. Her hushed voice accentuated the silence in the room.

I can still hear Anne's voice as she softly broke that silence and said, "Perhaps the reason you've never heard that story before is because you've never talked to the <u>real</u> Santa Claus."

Other Books From Blue Sky Marketing Inc.

101 Questions About Santa Claus, with answers accurately recorded by Bob Litak.
Santa answers such puzzling questions as "How are Santa's reindeer able to fly?" and "What if a home has no chimney?"
Hardcover, 128 pages; 5x7, ISBN: 0-911493-23-9

The Home Owner's Journal: What I Did & When I Did It, by Colleen Jenkins.
The best-selling, easiest-to-use home record keeping book on the market.
Softcover (spiral binding), 136 pages, 6x9, ISBN: 0-911493-11-5

31 Days to RUIN Your Relationship, by Tricia Seymour & Rusty Barrier.
Tongue-in-cheek (reverse psychology) book of laugh-out-loud "affirmations."
Softcover, 80 pages, 6x4, ISBN: 0-911493-21-2

31 Days to INCREASE Your Stress, by Tricia Seymour.
Tongue-in-cheek (reverse psychology) book of laugh-out-loud "affirmations."
Softcover, 80 pages, 6x4, ISBN: 0-911493-19-0

It's So Cold In Minnesota... by Bonnie Stewart & Cathy McGlynn.
Hilarious, best-selling regional book poking fun at Minnesota winters.
Softcover, 6x4, 96 pages, ISBN: 0-911493-18-2

It's So Cold In Wisconsin..., by Bonnie Stewart & Cathy McGlynn.
Hilarious, new regional book poking fun at Wisconsin winters.
Softcover, 6x4, 96 pages, ISBN: 0-911493-20-4

Vacation Getaway: A Journal for Your Travel Memories.
With 15 pocket pages, it's the best-designed, best valued travel journal on the market.
Softcover (wire spiral binding), 36 pages (including pockets), 5x9, ISBN: 0-9633573-0-1

The Family Memory Book: Highlights of Our Times Together, by Judy Lawrence.
Easy-to-use, fill-in-the-blank book for recording highlights of family celebrations & holidays.
Hardcover, 96 pages, 7x10, ISBN: 0-911493-13-1

Our Family Memories: Highlights of Our Times Together, by Judy Lawrence.
Leather-like, embossed version of Family Memory Book.
Hardcover, 96 pages, 7x10, ISBN: 0-911493-14-X

Money & Time-Saving Household Hints, from The Leader-Post Carrier Foundation.
Over 1,000 clever, useful, and sometimes startling solutions to everyday problems.
Softcover, 128 pages, 6x9, ISBN: 0-911493-15-8

Other Books From Blue Sky Marketing Inc.
Continued

The Weekly Menu Planner & Shopping List.
The simple and easy way to plan your meals and shopping.
52 weekly sheets, 8.5x11, ISBN: 0-911493-05-0

The Bridal Shower Journal.
Keepsake for recording shower gifts & memories.
Includes 25 Thank You cards & envelopes.
Sturdy softcover with spiral wire binding, 22 pages (including 6 pockets), 7x10, ISBN: 0-9633573-2-8

Our Honeymoon: A Journal of Romantic Memories.
With 15 pocket pages, it's the best-designed, best valued honeymoon journal on the market.
Softcover (plastic comb binding), 36 pages (including pockets), 5x9, ISBN: 0-9633573-1-X